Hafro and The Wicked Leech

Peggy Flo

Charles Barry

MAPLE
PUBLISHERS

Hafro & The Wicked Leech

Author: Peggy Flo

Copyright © Peggy Flo (2022)

Illustrated by Charles Barry

The right of Peggy Flo to be identified as author of this work has been asserted by the author in accordance with section 77 and 78 of the Copyright, Designs and Patents Act 1988.

First Published in 2022

ISBN: 978-1-915492-24-1 (Paperback)
978-1-915492-25-8 (Hardback)
978-1-915492-26-5 (Ebook)

Book layout by:

White Magic Studios

www.whitemagicstudios.co.uk

Published by:

Maple Publishers

1 Brunel Way,

Slough,

SL1 1FQ, UK

www.maplepublishers.com

A CIP catalogue record for this title is available from the British Library.

A big thank you to

Layla Fayers, aged 8, class 4,

who kindly proof read the book and loved it!

Thank you to family and friends for support

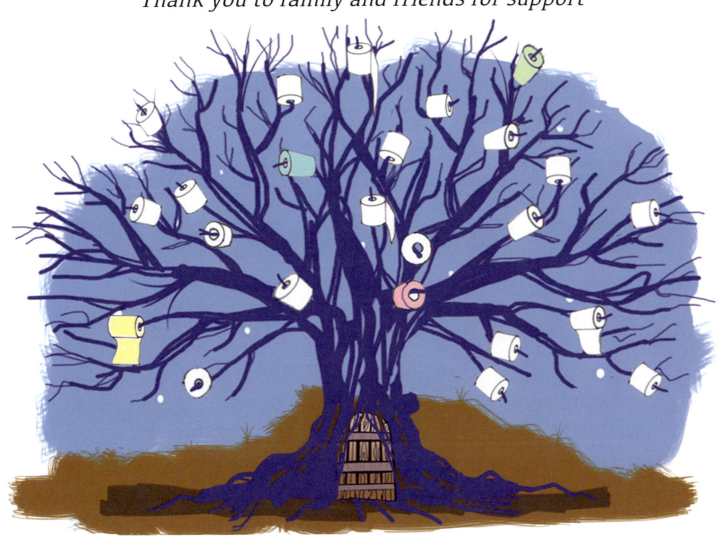

Hafro was new to the woodland,

He came from a land far away.

A strange looking creature. A frog or a hare?

Could be both, but it's quite hard to say.

His back legs are long and so furry,

The front ones are shaped like a frog.

He has very large eyes, an inflatable chest,

And will never get stuck in a bog.

He lives in a hole that is dark, slightly damp,

In the base of a bogaloo tree.

He wants to make friends, bake biscuits and

cakes,

And invite woodland creatures for tea.

Every morning he jumped from his

hollow,

To greet animals walking the track.

They ran to avoid his large googly eyes,

And most thought they'd never go back.

He was saddened that nobody liked him,

And dreamt he could just be the same,

If only they'd stop and say "hi, how are you?"

And invite him to join in a game.

His favourite fun is to play Hide and Seek,

He once went and hid by a wall,

He shouted, gave clues to reveal his place,

But nobody found him at all.

He walked in the woodland at night time,

To avoid being stared at and teased.

If only they knew how friendly he was,

Would make him so happy and pleased.

On one of his nightly excursions,

He heard a disturbing loud shriek.

An animal hurt, or stuck in a hole,

He drew closer to have a quick peek.

In the thick of a tree was a Blipso.

Held tight by a Thorny nosed Leech,

The tree in a river, so deep and so wide,

Other animals just couldn't reach.

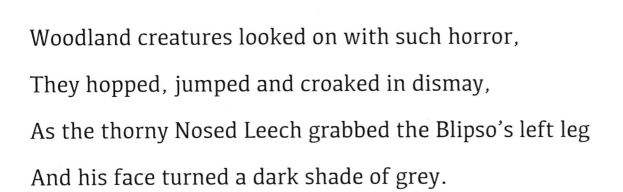

Woodland creatures looked on with such horror,

They hopped, jumped and croaked in dismay,

As the thorny Nosed Leech grabbed the Blipso's left leg

And his face turned a dark shade of grey.

Hafro was there in an instant.

With long legs he lept high in the air.

Jumped into the river, inflated his chest,

And then swam without even a care.

In moments he'd reached the tree branches,

That hung in the water so low,

Grasped hold of the leaves,

did a flip in the air,

Snatched the Blipso in one easy go.

The Thorny Nosed Leech toppled over,

Head first in the river he fell.

Washed away, out of sight, but will he return?

It's thought he now lives in a well.

The Blipso was cold and so shaken.

He held tight on to Hafro's long ears.

As he swam the wide river, to safety again,

To loud clapping and deafening cheers.

The Blipso hugged Hafro and kissed him,

Soon after, as Hafro had feared,

Woodland folk turned away, took the young Blipso

home,

And in moments they'd all disappeared.

Poor Hafro was tired and lonely,

Loped back and crawled into his bed.

Happy he'd saved the young Blipso from harm,

"Good job Hafro" was all that he said.

Next morning he woke rather startled.

Loud noise near his Bogaloo tree.

Music and laughing - whatever was wrong?

He lifted himself up to see.

The creatures ouside held a banner.

"Thank you Hafro" he read on the sign.

He cautiously climbed from the Bogaloo tree,

But thought it would all be quite fine.

One by one, woodland animals patted his head,

They smiled and said "you're so brave,

To risk the wide river and Thorny Nosed Leech,

For the Blipso you managed to save."

They were sad for their rudeness and silence,

And realised they'd been so unkind.

So they made him a cake filled with acorns and nuts,

And anything else they could find.

Young Blipso ran up and hugged Hafro,

They danced and ate cake for a week.

Every day Hafro's smile is wider than wide,

And they all love to play Hide and Seek.

Hafro's tale is one of true kindness.

So maybe we'll never forget.

That everyone's different,

Let's smile and say "Hi",

To the friend we just haven't

yet met.

Chester

Oscar

THANK YOU HAFRO

Momo   Spotty   Chesney

Layla

Thank you to Hafro and his friends : -

Chester, Oscar, Momo, Chesney, Layla, Spotty and the Pinkasnubs

26

CPSIA information can be obtained
at www.ICGtesting.com
Printed in the USA
LVRC101018161022
730716LV00015B/892